LISTENING, UNDERSTANDING, REMEMBERING, VERBALIZING!

Jean Gilliam DeGaetano

Illustrations by Kevin M. Newman

Great Ideas for Teaching, Inc. • **P.O. Box 444** • **Wrightsville Beach, NC 28480**

ISBN 1-886143-46-3

LISTENING, UNDERSTANDING, REMEMBERING, VERBALIZING!

By Jean Gilliam DeGaetano
Illustrations by Kevin M. Newman

Designed for ages 6-8

Listening to a story, understanding its meaning, remembering the details, and then being able to verbalize answers to questions are essential steps in developing higher-level language skills and in progressing in academic learning. The four skills need to be <u>combined</u> in activities, recognizing that each skill is dependent on the others if children are to master higher-level language.

The goals of the unit are:

1. to be able to listen attentively to a story.
2. to understand the story.
3. to remember the details.
4. to be able to answer questions about the story.
5. to retell the story.

The short stories are to be read aloud to the students as they look at the pictures, utilizing both the visual and auditory channels of learning.

To determine how well the details have been retained; questions, sentence completions and answer choices are provided for each story. These should reinforce remembering the details and assist the students in the final step of retelling each story.

At the end of every four stories, a summary is presented to show how well the students have retained the details of all four stories. Again, both visual and auditory clues are presented to assist the students in remembering the details in all four stories.

Name: _____

LISTENING, UNDERSTANDING, REMEMBERING,
VERBALIZING!

Instructor's Worksheet

Directions: Before beginning, each student should be given a copy of the picture that corresponds to the instructor's worksheet. The students are to look at the picture as they listen to the story being read aloud. Utilizing both the visual and auditory channels simultaneously will aid the students in remembering the details of the story. The students are to answer the questions or complete the sentences as they are read aloud. Finally, the students should look at the picture and retell the story in their own words.

Story #1:

Molly is sick. She is lying in her bed. Yesterday, she ate too much candy. The candy was delicious. The problem is Molly ate too much of it. Now she has an upset stomach. Molly's mother did not know that Molly had eaten that much candy.

A. Will you help Molly explain what happened and why she is sick?

1. Is Molly sleepy or sick?

2. She is lying on her _____.

3. Molly's mother is not sure why Molly is _____.

4. Molly told her mom she thinks she ate too much _____.

5. Did Molly eat the candy today or yesterday?

6. Her mother asked her where she hurts and Molly pointed to her _____.

7. Molly said she ate too much because the candy was _____.

8. Did Molly eat a small amount of candy or too much candy?

9. Is Molly's stomach twisted or upset?

10. Molly's mother told her to try to sleep and maybe she will feel _____.

B. Look at the picture and retell the story.

Name: _____

LISTENING, UNDERSTANDING, REMEMBERING, VERBALIZING!

Instructor's Worksheet

Directions: Before beginning, each student should be given a copy of the picture that corresponds to the instructor's worksheet. The students are to look at the picture as they listen to the story being read aloud. Utilizing both the visual and auditory channels simultaneously will aid the students in remembering the details of the story. The students are to answer the questions or complete the sentences as they are read aloud. Finally, the students should look at the picture and retell the story in their own words.

Story #2:

Today, there is a special music program at school. Three newspaper reporters have come to take pictures to put in the newspaper. They have written down all the children's names and information about the music program. They have told the children to look in the newspaper tomorrow to see their pictures.

A. Will you help the children explain what happened today at school?

1. Are the children having a music program or an art program?

2. Where is the music program being held?

3. Who came to the program? Why did the newspaper reporters come?

4. How many reporters came to the program?

5. They used their cameras to take _____.

6. Where are they going to put the pictures?

7. Did the reporters write down the children's names or pets' names?

8. What else did the reporters write down?

9. Where will the children look to see their pictures?

10. When will the pictures be in the newspaper?

B. Look at the picture and retell the story.

LISTENING, UNDERSTANDING, REMEMBERING, VERBALIZING!

Name: _____

LISTENING, UNDERSTANDING, REMEMBERING,
VERBALIZING!

Instructor's Worksheet

Directions: Before beginning, each student should be given a copy of the picture that corresponds to the instructor's worksheet. The students are to look at the picture as they listen to the story being read aloud. Utilizing both the visual and auditory channels simultaneously will aid the students in remembering the details of the story. The students are to answer the questions or complete the sentences as they are read aloud. Finally, the students should look at the picture and retell the story in their own words.

Story #3:

Mr. Jones is a teacher. He is taking a hike in the woods to see if this trail will be a good nature walk for his students. Mr. Jones passes a cave. Suddenly, he sees four eyes. The problem is he cannot see in the cave and doesn't know if the eyes belong to bears, owls, cats or raccoons. He hurries away very fast.

A. Will you help Mr. Jones explain what he saw?

1. Is Mr. Jones a teacher or a doctor?

2. Mr. Jones is walking in the _____.

3. Why was he taking a hike in the woods?

4. Did he pass by a big cave or a little pond?

5. Inside the cave, he sees four _____.

6. Can Mr. Jones see inside the cave?

7. Does Mr. Jones know what is inside the cave?

8. What kind of animals do you think are inside the cave?

9. Did Mr. Jones walk away from the cave slowly or did he hurry away?

10. Do you think he will take his students inside the cave? Why not?

B. Look at the picture and retell the story.

LISTENING, UNDERSTANDING, REMEMBERING, VERBALIZING!

Name: _____

Instructor's Worksheet

Directions: Before beginning, each student should be given a copy of the picture that corresponds to the instructor's worksheet. The students are to look at the picture as they listen to the story being read aloud. Utilizing both the visual and auditory channels simultaneously will aid the students in remembering the details of the story.   The students are to answer the questions or complete the sentences as they are read aloud.   Finally, the students should look at the picture and retell the story in their own words.

Story #4:

Michael saw some big red apples on an apple tree. He pulled one off and ate it. It was so good that he ate another one. Then he ate another one. Soon his stomach began to hurt. He sat down under the tree and thought, "I don't feel good. The apples were delicious but I ate too many. My tummy hurts."

A. Will you help Michael explain what happened?

1. What was on the tree?

2. Were the apples red or yellow?

3. Did Michael pick an apple off the tree or pick it up off the ground?

4. What did Michael do with the apple?

5. Did Michael eat just one apple?

6. Did Michael eat more than two apples?

7. Did Michael sit down under a tree or under an umbrella?

8. How did he feel after he ate the apples?

9. Did the apples taste delicious or did they taste sour?

10. Was something wrong with the apples or did Michael eat too many?

B. Look at the picture and retell the story.

LISTENING, UNDERSTANDING, REMEMBERING, VERBALIZING!

Name: _____

Story #1

Story #2

Story #3

Story #4

LISTENING, UNDERSTANDING, REMEMBERING, VERBALIZING!

Instructor's Worksheet   Remembering Stories 1-4

Directions: This summary activity worksheet should follow the four consecutive stories below. This review will determine if facts in the four stories have been retained. The students should have the student worksheet with the pictures in front of them as the questions are being read aloud. Students should take turns answering the questions.

Story #1   Story #2   Story #3   Story #4

1. Was Molly sleepy or sick?

2. Molly told her mom she thinks she ate too much _____.

3. Molly's mother asked her where she hurt and she pointed to her _____.

4. Did Molly eat a little bit or too much candy?

5. Were the children having a music program or an art program at school?

6. Who came to take pictures of the children's music program?

7. Did the reporters write down the children's names or their pets' names?

8. Where will the children look to see their pictures?

9. Why is Mr. Jones taking a walk in the woods?

10. Did Mr. Jones pass a big cave or a little pond?

11. Did Mr. Jones know what was inside the cave?

12. Did Mr. Jones walk away from the cave slowly or did he hurry away?

13. Did Michael pick the apples off the tree or pick them up off the ground?

14. Did Michael eat just one apple?

15. Did Michael eat three apples or ten apples?

16. Was something wrong with the apples or did Michael just eat too many?

Listening, Understanding, Remembering, Verbalizing!

Name: _____

Instructor's Worksheet

Directions: Before beginning, each student should be given a copy of the picture that corresponds to the instructor's worksheet. The students are to look at the picture as they listen to the story being read aloud. Utilizing both the visual and auditory channels simultaneously will aid the students in remembering the details of the story. The students are to answer the questions or complete the sentences as they are read aloud. Finally, the students should look at the picture and retell the story in their own words.

Story #5:

A cow was walking along eating grass. The cow saw two pigs playing in a mud puddle in their pigpen. The pigs asked the cow why she was eating grass. They told the cow they would not like to walk around eating grass all day. The cow said grass is her favorite food and eating grass is her favorite thing to do every day. The cow asked the pigs why they were rolling around in the mud. They said they love to roll in muddy puddles. The cow turned up her nose and said, "Ugh!"

A. Will you help Mrs. Cow explain about the pigs?

1. The cow was walking along eating _____.

2. What farm animals did the cow see?

3. What were the pigs doing?

4. The mud puddle was in the _____.

5. What is the cow's favorite thing to do all day?

6. Do pigs like to eat grass all day?

7. The pigs like to roll around in the _____.

8. Would the cow like to roll around in the mud all day?

9. Did the cow turn up her nose or turn up her ears?

10. Did the cow say anything when she left the pigs?

B. Look at the picture and retell the story.

Name: _____

LISTENING, UNDERSTANDING, REMEMBERING,
VERBALIZING!

Instructor's Worksheet

Directions: Before beginning, each student should be given a copy of the picture that corresponds to the instructor's worksheet. The students are to look at the picture as they listen to the story being read aloud. Utilizing both the visual and auditory channels simultaneously will aid the students in remembering the details of the story. The students are to answer the questions or complete the sentences as they are read aloud. Finally, the students should look at the picture and retell the story in their own words.

Story #6:

The clown is trying to teach his dog a new trick. The clown wants his dog to jump through the hoop, pick up the ball with its mouth and jump back through the hoop. The problem is the dog jumps through the hoop, picks up the ball and runs away with it. When the clown yells, "Come back! Come back!," the dog just lies down on the ground and chews the ball.

A. Will you help the clown explain what his dog does?

1. What is the clown trying to teach his dog?

2. What is the clown holding in his hand?

3. Is the dog supposed to roll through the hoop or jump through the hoop?

4. After the dog jumps through the hoop, it is supposed to pick up a _____.

5. Does the dog pick up the ball with its mouth or its paws?

6. What is the dog supposed to do with the ball after it picks it up?

7. Instead of bringing the ball back, what does the dog do with the ball?

8. What did the clown yell at the dog?

9. Do you think the dog likes to chew the ball?

10. Did the dog learn to do the new trick?

B. Look at the picture and retell the story.

LISTENING, UNDERSTANDING, REMEMBERING, VERBALIZING!

Name: _____

LISTENING, UNDERSTANDING, REMEMBERING, VERBALIZING!

Instructor's Worksheet

Directions: Before beginning, each student should be given a copy of the picture that corresponds to the instructor's worksheet. The students are to look at the picture as they listen to the story being read aloud. Utilizing both the visual and auditory channels simultaneously will aid the students in remembering the details of the story. The students are to answer the questions or complete the sentences as they are read aloud. Finally, the students should look at the picture and retell the story in their own words.

Story #7:

Sam wants a "double decker" chocolate ice cream cone. A "double decker" is two big scoops of ice cream, with one scoop on top of the other. When Sam started licking the ice cream, he accidentally knocked off the top scoop. It fell in the dirt and that was the end of that. Sam was really sad and upset because chocolate ice cream is his favorite treat.

A. Will you help Sam explain what happened?

1. Did Sam want an ice cream cone or a bowl of ice cream?

2. What kind of ice cream cone did Sam want?

3. What does "double decker" mean?

4. Sam's favorite ice cream is _____.

5. Do people eat ice cream cones with spoons? How do they eat them?

6. What happened when Sam started licking the ice cream?

7. Did both scoops of ice cream fall off the cone?

8. The ice cream fell in the _____.

9. How did Sam feel when the ice cream fell in the dirt?

10. What is Sam's favorite treat?

B. Look at the picture and retell the story.

LISTENING, UNDERSTANDING, REMEMBERING, VERBALIZING!

Name: _____

LISTENING, UNDERSTANDING, REMEMBERING,
VERBALIZING!

Instructor's Worksheet

Directions: Before beginning, each student should be given a copy of the picture that corresponds to the instructor's worksheet. The students are to look at the picture as they listen to the story being read aloud. Utilizing both the visual and auditory channels simultaneously will aid the students in remembering the details of the story. The students are to answer the questions or complete the sentences as they are read aloud. Finally, the students should look at the picture and retell the story in their own words.

Story #8:

Ramon is a very good math student. He usually gets all the answers right. His teacher wrote the answers to the first two problems on the blackboard. Then the teacher asked Ramon to go to the blackboard and write the answers to the last two problems. She thought she handed him a piece of chalk but she handed him a crayon by mistake. Ramon could not write the answers. His teacher asked, "Ramon, do you not know the answers?" Ramon said, "Yes, I do, but I can't write them." His teacher saw that she had given him a crayon instead of chalk and everyone began to laugh.

A. Will you help Ramon explain what happened?

1. Ramon is very good at _____.

2. Does he usually get all the answers right?

3. What did the teacher write on the blackboard?

4. What did the teacher ask Ramon to do?

5. How many problems does Ramon need to solve?

6. Instead of giving Ramon a piece of chalk, she gave him a _____.

7. Could Ramon write the answers on the blackboard? Why not?

8. Do you think Ramon knows the answers to the problems?

9. What did he tell the teacher?

10. Did the children laugh or cry when they saw what the teacher had done?

B. Look at the picture and retell the story.

LISTENING, UNDERSTANDING, REMEMBERING, VERBALIZING!

Name: _____

Story #5

Story #6

Story #7

Story #8

LISTENING, UNDERSTANDING, REMEMBERING, VERBALIZING!

Instructor's Worksheet   Remembering Stories 5-8

Directions: This summary activity worksheet should follow the four consecutive stories below. This review will determine if facts in the four stories have been retained. The students should have the student worksheet with the pictures in front of them as the questions are being read aloud. Students should take turns answering the questions.

Story #5   Story #6   Story #7   Story #8

1. The cow was walking along eating _____.

2. What were the pigs doing when Mrs. Cow saw them?

3. Do pigs like to eat grass all day?

4. Would Mrs. Cow like to roll around in the mud all day?

5. What is the clown trying to teach his dog?

6. After the dog jumps through the hoop, it is supposed to pick up a _____.

7. What did the dog do with the ball?

8. Did the dog learn a new trick? Why not?

9. What kind of ice cream cone did Sam want?

10. Sam's favorite ice cream is _____.

11. What happened when Sam started licking the ice cream?

12. The ice cream fell in the _____.

13. Ramon is very good at _____.

14. What did the teacher ask Ramon to do?

15. Could Ramon write the answers on the blackboard? Why not?

16. Did the children laugh or cry when the teacher realized she gave Ramon a crayon?

Name: _____

LISTENING, UNDERSTANDING, REMEMBERING,
VERBALIZING!

Instructor's Worksheet

Directions: Before beginning, each student should be given a copy of the picture that corresponds to the instructor's worksheet. The students are to look at the picture as they listen to the story being read aloud. Utilizing both the visual and auditory channels simultaneously will aid the students in remembering the details of the story. The students are to answer the questions or complete the sentences as they are read aloud. Finally, the students should look at the picture and retell the story in their own words.

Story #9:

Cynthia is in the fourth grade. Her class was having a favorite pet day at school. Everyone was allowed to bring a pet. Cynthia's mom leaves for work early; therefore, she could not bring Cynthia's pet to school. Cynthia explained why she could not bring her pet and told the teacher she would draw a picture of her pet on the blackboard. She used a green piece of chalk to draw a picture of a cat.

A. Will you help Cynthia explain what she did for pet day?

1. What grade is Cynthia in?

2. What special day was it at Cynthia's school?

3. Were the children allowed to bring a pet or a toy to school?

4. Cynthia's mom leaves for work _____.

5. Did Cynthia bring her pet to school?

6. What did Cynthia tell her teacher?

7. Cynthia drew a picture of her pet on the _____.

8. What kind of pet does Cynthia have?

9. What did Cynthia use to draw the picture of the cat?

10. Does her cat have whiskers?

B. Look at the picture and retell the story.

Name: _____

Instructor's Worksheet

Directions: Before beginning, each student should be given a copy of the picture that corresponds to the instructor's worksheet. The students are to look at the picture as they listen to the story being read aloud. Utilizing both the visual and auditory channels simultaneously will aid the students in remembering the details of the story. The students are to answer the questions or complete the sentences as they are read aloud. Finally, the students should look at the picture and retell the story in their own words.

Story #10:

When Tony's alarm rang, he woke up. He climbed out of bed, washed his face and hands, dressed, made his bed and walked to the kitchen. When he walked into the kitchen, his mother was not cooking breakfast. His father was not drinking coffee and reading the newspaper and everything was very quiet. Tony wondered what was wrong. Where was everybody? He called to his mom and dad. They laughed and told him he had set his alarm by mistake. Today was not a school day. It was Saturday.

A. Will you help Tony explain what happened?

1. What happened when Tony's alarm rang?

2. What did Tony do when he woke up?

3. Did Tony walk to the kitchen before or after he dressed and made his bed?

4. Was anyone in the kitchen?

5. Was it noisy in the kitchen or very quiet?

6. What did Tony do when he did not see anyone in the kitchen?

7. Did his mom and dad laugh or cry when he called them?

8. What did Tony do by mistake?

9. Was today a school day?

10. What day was it?

B. Look at the picture and retell the story.

Name: _____

LISTENING, UNDERSTANDING, REMEMBERING,
VERBALIZING!

Instructor's Worksheet

Directions: Before beginning, each student should be given a copy of the picture that corresponds to the instructor's worksheet. The students are to look at the picture as they listen to the story being read aloud. Utilizing both the visual and auditory channels simultaneously will aid the students in remembering the details of the story. The students are to answer the questions or complete the sentences as they are read aloud. Finally, the students should look at the picture and retell the story in their own words.

Story #11:

Judd and Mark walked to the pond in the park. The water was not deep so the children were allowed to play there. They decided to stand on the rocks in the pond, even though they had told their mothers they would not get wet. Suddenly, a frog leaped high in the air to catch a fly. Judd was so startled and surprised that he fell off the rock into the water. Of course, his clothes got soaking wet.

A. Will you help Judd explain to his mother how he got wet?

1. Where did Judd and Mark walk?

2. Was the pond shallow or deep?

3. What did Judd and Mark decide to stand on?

4. What did they tell their mothers before they went to the park?

5. What leaped out of the water?

6. The frog leaped high in the air to catch a _____.

7. Who was startled and surprised?

8. Because he was startled and surprised, Judd fell off the _____.

9. What happened to his clothes?

10. Did Mark get wet?

B. Look at the picture and retell the story.

TINK

Instructor's Worksheet

Directions: Before beginning, each student should be given a copy of the picture that corresponds to the instructor's worksheet. The students are to look at the picture as they listen to the story being read aloud. Utilizing both the visual and auditory channels simultaneously will aid the students in remembering the details of the story. The students are to answer the questions or complete the sentences as they are read aloud. Finally, the students should look at the picture and retell the story in their own words.

Story #12:

Today, Ted went with his class to visit a farm. The farmer told the children a blacksmith was putting new horseshoes on the farm horses and they could watch. The horseshoes are made of iron and they are nailed to the horses' hooves. They keep the horses' hooves from breaking or wearing down when the horses work or walk on hard roads. The children wanted to know if they hurt the horses when they were nailed on. The farmer said, "No, and they help protect the hooves like shoes help protect children's feet."

A. Will you help Ted explain what he saw today?

1. Where did Ted go to visit?

2. Did Ted go to the farm with his class or his family?

3. A person who puts horseshoes on a horse is called a _____.

4. Did the farmer tell the children they could watch the blacksmith?

5. What are horseshoes made of?

6. Where does a blacksmith nail the horseshoes?

7. Horses' feet are called _____.

8. Do horseshoes protect a horse's hooves or legs?

9. Why do horses need horseshoes?

10. Children do not wear horseshoes, they wear _____.

B. Look at the picture and retell the story.

LISTENING, UNDERSTANDING, REMEMBERING, VERBALIZING!

Story #9

Story #10

Story #11

Story #12

Instructor's Worksheet   Remembering Stories 9-12

Directions: This summary activity worksheet should follow the four consecutive stories below. This review will determine if facts in the four stories have been retained. The students should have the student worksheet with the pictures in front of them as the questions are being read aloud. Students should take turns answering the questions.

Story #9   Story #10   Story #11   Story #12

1. What special day was it at Cynthia's school?

2. Did Cynthia bring her pet to school? Why not?

3. What did Cynthia tell her teacher?

4. What kind of pet does Cynthia have?

5. What did Tony do when he woke up?

6. Did Tony walk to the kitchen before or after he dressed and made his bed?

7. Was anyone in the kitchen when Tony went in?

8. What did Tony do by mistake?

9. Where did Judd and Mark walk?

10. What did Judd and Mark tell their mothers before they went to the park?

11. What leaped out of the water and startled Judd?

12. What happened to Judd's clothes?

13. Did Ted go to the farm with his class or his family?

14. What was the blacksmith putting on the horses?

15. What do you call a horse's foot?

16. Why does a horse wear horseshoes?

Listening, Understanding, Remembering, Verbalizing!

Name: _____

LISTENING, UNDERSTANDING, REMEMBERING,
VERBALIZING!

Instructor's Worksheet

Directions: Before beginning, each student should be given a copy of the picture that corresponds to the instructor's worksheet. The students are to look at the picture as they listen to the story being read aloud. Utilizing both the visual and auditory channels simultaneously will aid the students in remembering the details of the story.   The students are to answer the questions or complete the sentences as they are read aloud.   Finally, the students should look at the picture and retell the story in their own words.

Story #13:

Today, Andre's teacher read a story about a friendly giant. It was a make-believe story, of course, but Andre loves make-believe stories about giants, fairies, monsters and ghosts. This friendly giant accidentally stepped on someone's house. His foot went through the roof and was stuck in the house. He carefully took his foot out of the house, fixed the roof like new and put the house back where it was before he stepped on it. The people thanked him. It was a good story.

A. Will you help Andre tell the story about the giant?

1. What special thing did Andre's teacher do today?

2. The story was about a friendly _____.

3. Was the story a make-believe story or a real story?

4. What kind of make-believe characters does Andre like?

5. In the story, what did the friendly giant do?

6. What happened to the house after the giant stepped on it?

7. Did the giant fix the roof?

8. What did he do with the house after he fixed the roof?

9. What did the people say after he fixed the house?

10. Did Andre like the story?

B. Look at the picture and retell the story.

LISTENING, UNDERSTANDING, REMEMBERING, VERBALIZING!

LISTENING, UNDERSTANDING, REMEMBERING,
VERBALIZING!

Instructor's Worksheet

Directions: Before beginning, each student should be given a copy of the picture that corresponds to the instructor's worksheet. The students are to look at the picture as they listen to the story being read aloud. Utilizing both the visual and auditory channels simultaneously will aid the students in remembering the details of the story. The students are to answer the questions or complete the sentences as they are read aloud. Finally, the students should look at the picture and retell the story in their own words.

Story #14:

Billy is at the beach with his family. The lifeguard told all the swimmers to watch out for jellyfish in the water. Jellyfish are not always around the swimmers' area but today they are. Billy laughed and said, "No silly jellyfish is going to hurt me." His mother warned him to listen to the lifeguard and be careful. If the other swimmers saw a jellyfish, they moved away from it. Billy just laughed and swam close to it. As you might have guessed, a jellyfish reached over to Billy with one of its tentacles and gave Billy a sting on his shoulder. Billy yelled, "Ouch" and swam away as fast as he could.

A. Will you help Billy explain about the jellyfish?

1. Where did Billy and his family go?

2. What did the lifeguard tell Billy?

3. What did Billy do when the lifeguard told him about the jellyfish?

4. Billy's mother told him to be _____.

5. What did the other swimmers do when they saw the jellyfish?

6. Did Billy swim away from the jellyfish or swim near it?

7. The jellyfish reached over to Billy and touched him with one of its _____.

8. Did the jellyfish tickle Billy or sting him?

9. What did Billy yell when the jellyfish stung him?

10. What did Billy do after the jellyfish stung him?

B. Look at the picture and retell the story.

LISTENING, UNDERSTANDING, REMEMBERING, VERBALIZING!

Instructor's Worksheet

Directions: Before beginning, each student should be given a copy of the picture that corresponds to the instructor's worksheet. The students are to look at the picture as they listen to the story being read aloud. Utilizing both the visual and auditory channels simultaneously will aid the students in remembering the details of the story.   The students are to answer the questions or complete the sentences as they are read aloud.   Finally, the students should look at the picture and retell the story in their own words.

Story #15:

Hugo looked out the window and saw that lots of snow had fallen during the night. Today, he will do his favorite thing in the snow. Is it sledding? Is it skiing? Is it building a fort? Hugo said it was none of these. His favorite thing is to put on a warm coat and to take a long walk in the snow. He likes to make lots of footprints in the snow and let snowflakes fall on his face.

A. Will you explain what Hugo likes to do in the snow?

1. Did Hugo look out of a window or out of a door?

2. What had fallen during the night?

3. Is sledding Hugo's favorite thing to do in the snow?

4. Is skiing Hugo's favorite thing to do in the snow?

5. Is building a snowfort Hugo's favorite thing to do in the snow?

6. What is Hugo's favorite thing to do?

7. When he walks in the snow he likes to wear a warm _____.

8. When Hugo walks in the snow his feet make _____.

9. When it snows, do raindrops or snowflakes fall from the sky?

10. What does Hugo like to have fall on his face?

B. Look at the picture and retell the story.

LISTENING, UNDERSTANDING, REMEMBERING, VERBALIZING!

Name: _____

LISTENING, UNDERSTANDING, REMEMBERING, VERBALIZING!

Instructor's Worksheet

Directions: Before beginning, each student should be given a copy of the picture that corresponds to the instructor's worksheet. The students are to look at the picture as they listen to the story being read aloud. Utilizing both the visual and auditory channels simultaneously will aid the students in remembering the details of the story. The students are to answer the questions or complete the sentences as they are read aloud. Finally, the students should look at the picture and retell the story in their own words.

Story #16:

On this hot summer day, Mr. Jones is running a ten-mile race. He has been practicing every day to get ready for the race. All the runners wear shorts, sleeveless shirts and running shoes. The number on Mr. Jones's shirt is eight. The winner of the race is going to win a new mountain bike. The winner is the runner who gets to the finish line first and breaks the ribbon.

A. Will you explain about the race?

1. What kind of day is it today?

2. What is Mr. Jones doing?

3. How many miles long is the race?

4. What has Mr. Jones been doing to get ready for the race?

5. Do the runners wear long sleeved shirts or sleeveless shirts?

6. On their feet, the runners wear running _____.

7. What number is on Mr. Jones's shirt?

8. What prize will the winner get?

9. The winner is the runner who is the first person to cross the _____.

10. Does the winner break a ribbon or board when crossing the finish line?

B. Look at the picture and retell the story.

LISTENING, UNDERSTANDING, REMEMBERING, VERBALIZING!

Name: _____

Story #13

Story #14

Story #15

Story #16

LISTENING, UNDERSTANDING, REMEMBERING, VERBALIZING!

Instructor's Worksheet   Remembering Stories 13-16

Directions: This summary activity worksheet should follow the four consecutive stories below. This review will determine if facts in the four stories have been retained. The students should have the student worksheet with the pictures in front of them as the questions are being read aloud. Students should take turns answering the questions.

Story #13

Story #14

Story #15

Story #16

1. Andre's teacher read a special story about a _____.

2. What kind of make-believe characters does Andre like?

3. In the story, what did the friendly giant do?

4. What did the giant do with the house after he fixed the roof?

5. What did the lifeguard tell Billy?

6. Did Billy swim away from the jellyfish or swim near it?

7. Did the jellyfish tickle Billy or sting him?

8. What did Billy do after the jellyfish stung him?

9. When Hugo looked out the window, what did he see?

10. What is Hugo's favorite thing to do in the snow?

11. When he walks in the snow, what does Hugo wear?

12. What does Hugo like to have fall on his face?

13. What kind of race is Mr. Jones running in?

14. What number is on Mr. Jones's shirt?

15. What prize will the winner of the race receive?

16. Who wins the race?

Listening, Understanding, Remembering,
Verbalizing!

LISTENING, UNDERSTANDING, REMEMBERING,
VERBALIZING!

Instructor's Worksheet

Directions: Before beginning, each student should be given a copy of the picture that corresponds to the instructor's worksheet. The students are to look at the picture as they listen to the story being read aloud. Utilizing both the visual and auditory channels simultaneously will aid the students in remembering the details of the story. The students are to answer the questions or complete the sentences as they are read aloud. Finally, the students should look at the picture and retell the story in their own words.

Story #17:

Carla's mother wants Carla to get up because they are leaving very early this morning to go on vacation. Carla said, "It isn't morning yet. I want to stay in bed." Carla's mother said, "The sun is just coming up and it is getting light outside." Carla said, "I can't see the sun."
Her mom opened the blinds and Carla saw the sun starting to shine. "OK," she said, "I'm getting up now. I'm ready to go on vacation."

A. Will you explain why Carla didn't want to get up?

1. Who wants Carla to get up early this morning?

2. Why does Carla's mother want her to get up early?

3. Does Carla want to get out of bed?

4. Why doesn't Carla want to get up?

5. What did Carla's mother say to her?

6. Could Carla see the sun coming up? Why not?

7. Did Carla's mother open the blinds or the window?

8. When Carla's mother opened the blinds, Carla could see the _____.

9. What did Carla decide to do when she saw the sun shining?

10. Was she ready to go on vacation?

B. Look at the picture and retell the story.

Name: _____

Instructor's Worksheet

Directions: Before beginning, each student should be given a copy of the picture that corresponds to the instructor's worksheet. The students are to look at the picture as they listen to the story being read aloud. Utilizing both the visual and auditory channels simultaneously will aid the students in remembering the details of the story. The students are to answer the questions or complete the sentences as they are read aloud. Finally, the students should look at the picture and retell the story in their own words.

Story #18:

Scott was out in his rowboat when he heard someone call out, "Help!" Scott yelled back, "I'm coming to help you." He quickly rowed his boat near the lady and threw a life preserver to her. Life preservers float in the water and people hold on to them so they float on top of the water. Scott pulled the lady to his boat with the long rope that was attached to the life preserver and she climbed into the boat.

A. Will you explain what Scott did with the life preserver?

1. Was Scott in his rowboat or his sailboat?

2. What did he hear someone yell?

3. Did Scott decide to help the lady?

4. What did he do?

5. Did he throw a life preserver or a pillow to her?

6. Life preservers float on top of the _____.

7. What does a person do with a life preserver?

8. What did Scott use to pull the lady to his boat?

9. The rope was attached to the _____.

10. What did the lady do when she reached the boat?

B. Look at the picture and retell the story.

Name: _____

LISTENING, UNDERSTANDING, REMEMBERING,
VERBALIZING!

Instructor's Worksheet

Directions: Before beginning, each student should be given a copy of the picture that corresponds to the instructor's worksheet. The students are to look at the picture as they listen to the story being read aloud. Utilizing both the visual and auditory channels simultaneously will aid the students in remembering the details of the story. The students are to answer the questions or complete the sentences as they are read aloud. Finally, the students should look at the picture and retell the story in their own words.

Story #19:

It is a rainy day and Millie's mother needs bread from the store but her car will not start. She says, "I can't make sandwiches for lunch because I have no bread." Millie's grandmother lives next door. Millie told her mother she would walk next door to her grandmother's house to borrow bread. She put on her raincoat and boots and took an umbrella so she would not get wet. She took a plastic bag to put the bread slices in so they would not get wet either.

A. Will you help Millie tell her grandmother why she has walked to her house in the rain?

1. What kind of day is it?

2. What does Millie's mother need from the store?

3. Why can't Millie's mother drive to the store?

4. Millie's mother needs bread so that she can make _____.

5. Is Millie's mother making sandwiches for lunch or dinner?

6. Who lives next door to Millie?

7. What did Millie tell her mother she would do?

8. What did Millie put on so that she would not get her clothes and shoes wet?

9. What else did Millie use so that she would not get wet?

10. What did Millie take with her so that the bread would not get wet?

B. Look at the picture and retell the story.

Name: _____

Instructor's Worksheet

Directions: Before beginning, each student should be given a copy of the picture that corresponds to the instructor's worksheet. The students are to look at the picture as they listen to the story being read aloud. Utilizing both the visual and auditory channels simultaneously will aid the students in remembering the details of the story. The students are to answer the questions or complete the sentences as they are read aloud. Finally, the students should look at the picture and retell the story in their own words.

Story #20:

"Oh no!" said George's dad. "Garbage is all over our yard. What a mess!" His dad wondered who had turned over the garbage can. It was a mystery. It rained last night so his dad went outside to see if he could see any footprints in the mud. When he came back in the house, he said he knew what, not who, had tipped over the garbage can. There were little animal paw prints in the mud all around the garbage. The paw prints belonged to raccoons!

A. Will you help George's dad explain what happened?

1. What was all over the yard?

2. Did George's dad know what had happened?

3. How did the garbage get out of the can?

4. Did it rain or snow last night?

5. What was his dad looking for in the mud?

6. When he came back inside, did he know what had happened to the garbage can?

7. Did dad find footprints or paw prints in the mud?

8. Were the paw prints big or little?

9. What did the paw prints belong to?

B. Look at the picture and retell the story.

LISTENING, UNDERSTANDING, REMEMBERING, VERBALIZING!

Name: _____

Story #17

Story #18

Story #19

Story #20

LISTENING, UNDERSTANDING, REMEMBERING,
VERBALIZING!

Instructor's Worksheet   Remembering Stories 17-20

Directions: This summary activity worksheet should follow the four consecutive stories below. This review will determine if facts in the four stories have been retained. The students should have the student worksheet with the pictures in front of them as the questions are being read aloud. Students should take turns answering the questions.

Story #17

Story #18

Story #19

Story #20

1. Why does Carla's mother want her to get up early?

2. Why doesn't Carla want to get up?

3. Why did Carla's mother open the blinds?

4. What did Carla do when she saw the sun coming up?

5. Where was Scott when he heard someone yell help?

6. What did Scott throw to the lady?

7. What did the lady do with the life preserver?

8. What did the lady do when she reached Scott's boat?

9. What does Millie's mother need from the store?

10. What did Millie tell her mother she would do?

11. What did Millie put on so she would not get wet?

12. What did Millie take with her so that the bread would not get wet?

13. What did George's dad see all over the yard?

14. How did the garbage get all over the yard?

15. What did George's dad see in the mud?

16. What did the paw prints belong to?

Listening, Understanding, Remembering, Verbalizing!

Name: _____

LISTENING, UNDERSTANDING, REMEMBERING, VERBALIZING!

Instructor's Worksheet

Directions: Before beginning, each student should be given a copy of the picture that corresponds to the instructor's worksheet. The students are to look at the picture as they listen to the story being read aloud. Utilizing both the visual and auditory channels simultaneously will aid the students in remembering the details of the story. The students are to answer the questions or complete the sentences as they are read aloud. Finally, the students should look at the picture and retell the story in their own words.

Story #21:

Juan has a new skateboard. He received it for his birthday. He also has a helmet and knee pads to keep from hurting his head and his knees if he falls. Juan rides his skateboard on his long driveway. It is a perfect place for skateboarding because it is very safe. Because it is safe, many of Juan's friends come over to his house to ride their skateboards on his driveway, also.

A. Will you help Juan explain about his new skateboard?

1. Juan has a new _____.

2. For what occasion did he get the skateboard?

3. What does he wear on his head?

4. What does he wear on his knees?

5. Why does he wear a helmet and knee pads?

6. Juan rides his skateboard on his _____.

7. Is the driveway long or short?

8. Is this a good place to ride a skateboard?

9. Why is it a good place to ride a skateboard?

10. Who else comes over to ride skateboards on Juan's driveway?

B. Look at the picture and retell the story.

Name: _____

LISTENING, UNDERSTANDING, REMEMBERING, VERBALIZING!

Instructor's Worksheet

Directions: Before beginning, each student should be given a copy of the picture that corresponds to the instructor's worksheet. The students are to look at the picture as they listen to the story being read aloud. Utilizing both the visual and auditory channels simultaneously will aid the students in remembering the details of the story. The students are to answer the questions or complete the sentences as they are read aloud. Finally, the students should look at the picture and retell the story in their own words.

Story #22:

Tommy is looking out the window and watching three squirrels playing in the backyard. They are picking up acorns. One of the squirrels is eating an acorn. One squirrel is hiding an acorn in the leaves on the ground. The other squirrel is taking an acorn to its nest in the tree. Tommy's mother asks him what he is watching.

A. Will you help Tommy explain what he is watching?

1. Is Tommy looking out of a window or door?

2. What does he see?

3. Where are the squirrels playing?

4. How many squirrels does he see?

5. Are the squirrels picking up acorns or pumpkins?

6. How many squirrels are eating acorns?

7. Where is one squirrel hiding an acorn?

8. One squirrel is taking an acorn to its _____.

9. Where is the squirrel's nest?

10. Who asked Tommy what he is watching?

B. Look at the picture and retell the story.

LISTENING, UNDERSTANDING, REMEMBERING, VERBALIZING!

Name: _____

LISTENING, UNDERSTANDING, REMEMBERING, VERBALIZING!

Instructor's Worksheet

Directions: Before beginning, each student should be given a copy of the picture that corresponds to the instructor's worksheet. The students are to look at the picture as they listen to the story being read aloud. Utilizing both the visual and auditory channels simultaneously will aid the students in remembering the details of the story.   The students are to answer the questions or complete the sentences as they are read aloud.   Finally, the students should look at the picture and retell the story in their own words.

Story #23:

Kippy's class is visiting a farm. The farmer is taking the children for a walk through a cornfield. They see a funny little man in the field. The farmer tells them it is not a real person. It is made of straw, has a painted face and is dressed in the farmer's old clothes. It is called a scarecrow. It is put in the cornfield to scare away the crows so that they will not eat the corn.

A. Will you help the children explain about the farm?

1. What place is Kippy's class visiting?

2. Who is taking the children for a walk?

3. Where are the children taking a walk?

4. What do they see in the field?

5. It is not a real person because it is made of _____.

6. What kind of face does it have?

7. What do you call something that is made of straw, has a painted face and wears old farm clothes?

8. Why did the farmer put a scarecrow in a field?

9. What kind of birds does the scarecrow scare away?

10. The scarecrow scares away the crows so they will not eat the _____.

B. Look at the picture and retell the story.

LISTENING, UNDERSTANDING, REMEMBERING, VERBALIZING!

Name: _____

Instructor's Worksheet

Directions: Before beginning, each student should be given a copy of the picture that corresponds to the instructor's worksheet. The students are to look at the picture as they listen to the story being read aloud. Utilizing both the visual and auditory channels simultaneously will aid the students in remembering the details of the story. The students are to answer the questions or complete the sentences as they are read aloud. Finally, the students should look at the picture and retell the story in their own words.

Story #24:

Sue has on her roller skates. She asked her mother if she could skate on the sidewalk. Her mother told her she could as soon as she skates well enough so that she does not have to hold on to anything to keep from falling. Sue told her mother she had a surprise for her; she could already skate without holding on to anything. Her mom smiled as Sue skated up and down the sidewalk.

A. Will you help Sue explain to her mother what she would like to do?

1. Sue is wearing a pair of _____.

2. Where does she want to skate?

3. What did Sue ask her mother?

4. What did her mother tell her?

5. Does Sue have a surprise for her mother?

6. What was the surprise?

7. Did Sue fall down?

8. Was Sue's mom happy or sad that Sue could skate without holding on?

9. Did Sue skate up and down the sidewalk or the road?

10. Do you think Sue is a good skater?

B. Look at the picture and retell the story.

Name: _____

Story #21

Story #22

Story #23

Story #24

LISTENING, UNDERSTANDING, REMEMBERING, VERBALIZING!

Instructor's Worksheet   Remembering Stories 21-24

Directions: This summary activity worksheet should follow the four consecutive stories below. This review will determine if facts in the four stories have been retained. The students should have the student worksheet with the pictures in front of them as the questions are being read aloud. Students should take turns answering the questions.

| Story #21 | Story #22 | Story #23 | Story #24 |

1. What did Juan get for his birthday?

2. Why does Juan wear a helmet and knee pads?

3. Where does Juan ride his skateboard?

4. Who else comes over and rides skateboards on Juan's driveway?

5. What did Tommy see when he looked out the window?

6. What did Tommy see the squirrels pick up?

7. Where was one squirrel hiding an acorn?

8. What were the other two squirrels doing?

9. What place was Kippy's class visiting?

10. What did Kippy and his classmates see in the field?

11. What is a scarecrow made of?

12. What kind of birds does the scarecrow scare away?

13. What is Sue wearing on her feet?

14. Where does Sue want to skate?

15. What did Sue's mother tell her?

16. What did Sue tell her mother that made her happy?

Listening, Understanding, Remembering, Verbalizing!

Instructor's Worksheet

Directions: Before beginning, each student should be given a copy of the picture that corresponds to the instructor's worksheet. The students are to look at the picture as they listen to the story being read aloud. Utilizing both the visual and auditory channels simultaneously will aid the students in remembering the details of the story. The students are to answer the questions or complete the sentences as they are read aloud. Finally, the students should look at the picture and retell the story in their own words.

Story #25:

Mrs. Johnson's class is studying clothing and how cloth is made. Jane's dad is a sheep shearer. He brought a sheep with a very thick coat of wool to the class. The wool is called fleece. Jane's dad sheared off all the wool with a pair of shears. The sheep did not mind at all because now it can start growing new fleece. All the fleece will be sent to spinners to make wool for sweaters, skirts, pants and coats.

A. Will you help explain what Jane's dad showed her class?

1. What is Mrs. Johnson's class studying?

2. What job does Jane's dad do?

3. What animal did he bring to class?

4. Did the sheep have a thick or thin coat of wool?

5. The thick wool on a sheep is called _____.

6. What did Jane's dad do to the sheep?

7. Did the sheep mind when Jane's dad sheared off its fleece?

8. How will the sheep get a new fleece?

9. Where will the fleece be sent?

10. What can be made out of wool?

B. Look at the picture and retell the story.

Name: _____

LISTENING, UNDERSTANDING, REMEMBERING,
VERBALIZING!

Instructor's Worksheet

Directions: Before beginning, each student should be given a copy of the picture that corresponds to the instructor's worksheet. The students are to look at the picture as they listen to the story being read aloud. Utilizing both the visual and auditory channels simultaneously will aid the students in remembering the details of the story. The students are to answer the questions or complete the sentences as they are read aloud. Finally, the students should look at the picture and retell the story in their own words.

Story #26:

Nick always wanted to build a tree house in the big tree in his backyard. One day his dad brought home some lumber in his truck. He told Nick it was for his tree house. It took Nick and his dad all day to build the tree house. It had a roof and a door. Nick's dad said he could use his wooden paint ladder to climb up to the tree house.

A. Will you help explain what Nick and his dad did?

1. What has Nick always wanted to build?

2. Where will he build the tree house?

3. Is the tree in his front yard or backyard?

4. What did Nick's dad bring home?

5. He brought home the lumber in his _____.

6. Did it take them a half day or all day to build the tree house?

7. What does the tree house have on top of it?

8. Does the tree house have a door?

9. Nick's dad said he could use his _____ to climb up to the tree house.

10. Is a tree house on the ground or up in a tree?

B. Look at the picture and retell the story.

Name: _____

LISTENING, UNDERSTANDING, REMEMBERING,
VERBALIZING!

Instructor's Worksheet

Directions: Before beginning, each student should be given a copy of the picture that corresponds to the instructor's worksheet. The students are to look at the picture as they listen to the story being read aloud. Utilizing both the visual and auditory channels simultaneously will aid the students in remembering the details of the story. The students are to answer the questions or complete the sentences as they are read aloud. Finally, the students should look at the picture and retell the story in their own words.

Story #27:

Ted was dressed and ready to go to school. He thought the weather was going to be warm today but when he looked out the window, he saw that it was a very windy day. Ted decided he would need to wear a coat or he would be cold waiting for the school bus. He took his coat off the hook, put it on and walked out the door to wait for his school bus.

A. Will you help explain why Ted decided to wear a coat today?

1. Ted was dressed and ready to go to _____.

2. Did he think the weather was going to be warm or cold?

3. Did he look out of the window or the door to check the weather?

4. What kind of day was it?

5. Ted decided he needed to wear a _____.

6. Why did he decide to wear his coat?

7. Where was his coat hanging?

8. Did he put the coat on or carry it on his arm?

9. Will Ted probably be warm now?

10. Will Ted wait for the school bus or his mother?

B. Look at the picture and retell the story.

Name: _____

LISTENING, UNDERSTANDING, REMEMBERING,
VERBALIZING!

Instructor's Worksheet

Directions: Before beginning, each student should be given a copy of the picture that corresponds to the instructor's worksheet. The students are to look at the picture as they listen to the story being read aloud. Utilizing both the visual and auditory channels simultaneously will aid the students in remembering the details of the story. The students are to answer the questions or complete the sentences as they are read aloud. Finally, the students should look at the picture and retell the story in their own words.

Story #28:

Kevin wanted to haul some bricks in his wagon so his little sister could build a play stove to cook on. When he started to pull his wagon, he discovered the handle was very loose. It needed a new screw. He found a new screw and a screwdriver in his dad's toolbox. After he put in the new screw, he used the wagon to haul the bricks for his sister. He also remembered to put the screwdriver back in his dad's toolbox.

A. Will you help explain how Kevin fixed his wagon?

1. What did Kevin want to haul in his wagon?

2. Who were the bricks for?

3. What did his little sister want to do with the bricks?

4. When he started to pull the wagon, he saw the handle was very _____.

5. What did the handle need?

6. Where did he look for a new screw?

7. What else did he get from his dad's toolbox?

8. Was the wagon fixed after he put in the new screw?

9. Do you think he made his sister happy?

10. Did he remember or forget to put the screwdriver back in his dad's toolbox?

B. Look at the picture and retell the story.

LISTENING, UNDERSTANDING, REMEMBERING, VERBALIZING!

Name: _____

Story #25

Story #26

Story #27

Story #28

LISTENING, UNDERSTANDING, REMEMBERING, VERBALIZING!

Instructor's Worksheet   Remembering Stories 25-28

Directions: This summary activity worksheet should follow the four consecutive stories below. This review will determine if facts in the four stories have been retained. The students should have the student worksheet with the pictures in front of them as the questions are being read aloud. Students should take turns answering the questions.

Story #25   Story #26   Story #27   Story #28

1. What is Jane's class studying?

2. What animal did Jane's dad bring to class?

3. What did Jane's dad do to the sheep?

4. What can be made of wool?

5. Where does Nick want to build his tree house?

6. Nick's dad brought home the lumber in his _____.

7. How long did it take to build the tree house?

8. What will Nick use to get up to his tree house?

9. Ted was dressed and ready to go to _____.

10. What did Ted see when he looked out the window?

11. Where was Ted's coat hanging?

12. What was Ted waiting for?

13. What did Kevin want to haul in his wagon?

14. What was wrong with the handle on Kevin's wagon?

15. What did Kevin need to fix the wagon?

16. Where did he find a screw and a screwdriver to fix the wagon?

Listening, Understanding, Remembering, Verbalizing!

Name: _____

LISTENING, UNDERSTANDING, REMEMBERING, VERBALIZING!

Instructor's Worksheet

Directions: Before beginning, each student should be given a copy of the picture that corresponds to the instructor's worksheet. The students are to look at the picture as they listen to the story being read aloud. Utilizing both the visual and auditory channels simultaneously will aid the students in remembering the details of the story. The students are to answer the questions or complete the sentences as they are read aloud. Finally, the students should look at the picture and retell the story in their own words.

Story #29:

Grandpa has a new camera. He wants to take some pictures to see how his new camera works. He wanted to take pictures of his dog, but it hid under the bed. He wanted to take pictures of the cat, but it ran behind the sofa. Grandpa went outside to take some pictures. A pretty butterfly flew by, but it would not stop fluttering. Grandpa was not able to take any pictures. He put the camera away until another day.

A. Will you help Grandpa explain why he did not take any pictures?

1. Who has a new camera?

2. What will he do with his camera?

3. Why did he want to take some pictures?

4. When he tried to take a picture of his dog, what did it do?

5. When he tried to take a picture of his cat, what did it do?

6. When Grandpa went outside, what flew by him?

7. Was it a pretty butterfly or an ugly butterfly?

8. Grandpa could not take a picture of the butterfly because it would not stop _____ .

9. Did Grandpa take any pictures?

10. What did Grandpa do with the camera?

B. Look at the picture and retell the story.

Instructor's Worksheet

Directions: Before beginning, each student should be given a copy of the picture that corresponds to the instructor's worksheet. The students are to look at the picture as they listen to the story being read aloud. Utilizing both the visual and auditory channels simultaneously will aid the students in remembering the details of the story. The students are to answer the questions or complete the sentences as they are read aloud. Finally, the students should look at the picture and retell the story in their own words.

Story #30:

Monica's little kitten gave a loud MEOW and rubbed against Monica's leg. Monica picked up her kitten and asked, "Do you want to sit on my lap?" Her kitten hopped down off her lap and gave another loud MEOW. Monica patted her kitten and asked, "Do you want to play?" The kitten gave a very loud MEOW and ran to the kitchen. Monica laughed. She knew what her kitten wanted. It was hungry. She filled its dish with cat food.

A. Will you help Monica explain why her kitten kept MEOWING?

1. Does Monica have a little dog or a little kitten?

2. What kind of sound did Monica's kitten make?

3. Monica's kitten rubbed against Monica's _____.

4. Did Monica's kitten want to stay on her lap?

5. Did Monica's kitten want to play?

6. The kitten did not want to play so it gave another loud _____.

7. Where did the kitten run?

8. When the kitten ran into the kitchen, Monica knew it was _____.

9. Did Monica give the kitten some milk or some food?

10. Where did Monica pour the cat food?

B. Look at the picture and retell the story.

Name: _____

LISTENING, UNDERSTANDING, REMEMBERING,
VERBALIZING!

Instructor's Worksheet

Directions: Before beginning, each student should be given a copy of the picture that corresponds to the instructor's worksheet. The students are to look at the picture as they listen to the story being read aloud. Utilizing both the visual and auditory channels simultaneously will aid the students in remembering the details of the story. The students are to answer the questions or complete the sentences as they are read aloud. Finally, the students should look at the picture and retell the story in their own words.

Story #31:

Valentine's Day is tomorrow and Millie wants to make valentines for her mom and dad. She has found some red paper in her desk drawer. That has made her happy because valentines are usually red and shaped like hearts. She cuts out two hearts with her scissors. After she cuts them out she uses glue to stick them on folded white paper. She thinks her mom and dad will be very happy with their valentines.

A. Will you help Millie explain how she made valentines for her mom and dad?

1. What day is tomorrow?

2. What does Millie want to make?

3. For whom does she want to make valentines?

4. What did Millie find in her desk drawer?

5. Valentines are usually red and shaped like _____.

6. How many red hearts did she cut out?

7. What did she use to cut out the hearts?

8. What color was the paper she stuck the hearts on?

9. What did she use to stick the hearts to the white paper?

10. Does Millie think her mom and dad will like their valentines?

B. Look at the picture and retell the story.

Instructor's Worksheet

Directions: Before beginning, each student should be given a copy of the picture that corresponds to the instructor's worksheet. The students are to look at the picture as they listen to the story being read aloud. Utilizing both the visual and auditory channels simultaneously will aid the students in remembering the details of the story. The students are to answer the questions or complete the sentences as they are read aloud. Finally, the students should look at the picture and retell the story in their own words.

Story #32:

Yesterday was a rainy day so Tina decided to play house. She put her Raggedy Ann in a wooden cradle and put a blanket over her. She asked her mom for some cookies and made a nice party table for her stuffed rabbit. Her mom let her put water in her little teapot and she pretended it was tea. Even though Tina pretended her rabbit was eating cookies, Tina really ate them all.

A. Will you help Tina explain about her tea party?

1. What kind of day was yesterday?

2. Tina decided to play _____.

3. What did she put in the cradle?

4. She covered her Raggedy Ann with a _____.

5. What did Tina ask her mom to give her for the party?

6. Tina made a nice tea party table for herself and her _____.

7. What did Tina's mom put in the teapot?

8. What did Tina pretend the water was?

9. Do you think the stuffed rabbit ate the cookies?

10. Who do you really think ate the cookies?

B. Look at the picture and retell the story.

LISTENING, UNDERSTANDING, REMEMBERING, VERBALIZING!

Name: _____

Story #29

Story #30

Story #31

Story #32

Instructor's Worksheet   Remembering Stories 29-32

Directions: This summary activity worksheet should follow the four consecutive stories below. This review will determine if facts in the four stories have been retained. The students should have the student worksheet with the pictures in front of them as the questions are being read aloud. Students should take turns answering the questions.

Story #29   Story #30   Story #31   Story #32

1. Grandpa has a new _____.

2. What did the dog do when Grandpa tried to take a picture of it?

3. What did the cat do when Grandpa tried to take a picture of it?

4. Did Grandpa take any pictures?

5. Does Monica have a little dog or a little kitten?

6. Did Monica's kitten want to play?

7. Where did the kitten run?

8. Did Monica give the kitten some milk or some food?

9. What did Millie want to make for her mom and dad?

10. Valentines are usually red and shaped like _____.

11. What did Millie use to cut out the hearts?

12. What did Millie use to stick the hearts to the white paper?

13. What did Tina put in the cradle?

14. What did Tina ask her mother for?

15. What did Tina pretend the water was?

16. Do you think the stuffed rabbit or Tina ate the cookies?

Listening, Understanding, Remembering, Verbalizing!

Name: _____

LISTENING, UNDERSTANDING, REMEMBERING,
VERBALIZING!

Instructor's Worksheet

Directions: Before beginning, each student should be given a copy of the picture that corresponds to the instructor's worksheet. The students are to look at the picture as they listen to the story being read aloud. Utilizing both the visual and auditory channels simultaneously will aid the students in remembering the details of the story. The students are to answer the questions or complete the sentences as they are read aloud. Finally, the students should look at the picture and retell the story in their own words.

Story #33:

Scotty was playing outside when he noticed that water was running out of the end of a hose. The water was making a big puddle. Scotty picked up his little shovel, walked over to the hose and started playing in the water puddle. Soon he had made a mud puddle out of the water puddle. Then he splashed and played in the puddle until he was covered in mud. What a mess he had made.

A. Will you help Scotty explain to his mother why he is muddy?

1. Was Scotty working or playing?

2. Was Scotty playing inside or outside?

3. What did he see running out of the hose?

4. The water was making a big _____.

5. What did Scotty pick up?

6. Where did he walk to?

7. What did he do when he reached the hose?

8. What did Scotty make out of the water puddle?

9. He splashed in the water until he was covered with _____.

10. Did Scotty make a mess?

B. Look at the picture and retell the story.

LISTENING, UNDERSTANDING, REMEMBERING, VERBALIZING!

Name: _____

LISTENING, UNDERSTANDING, REMEMBERING,
VERBALIZING!

Instructor's Worksheet

Directions: Before beginning, each student should be given a copy of the picture that corresponds to the instructor's worksheet. The students are to look at the picture as they listen to the story being read aloud. Utilizing both the visual and auditory channels simultaneously will aid the students in remembering the details of the story. The students are to answer the questions or complete the sentences as they are read aloud. Finally, the students should look at the picture and retell the story in their own words.

Story #34:

Damon wanted to help his dad. He decided to shovel the snow off the sidewalk before his dad came home from work. He went into the garage to get a big shovel. He shoveled and shoveled the snow, starting at the front steps and shoveling to the driveway. When he looked back, he said, "Oh, no! It is snowing so hard that the sidewalk is covered <u>again</u>. I will never finish."

A. Will you help explain why Damon might have to shovel the sidewalk again?

1. What did Damon want to do?

2. Did he decide to shovel or sweep the snow away?

3. Did he want to shovel the snow before or after his dad came home from work?

4. Where did he get his shovel?

5. Was it a big shovel or a little shovel?

6. Is Damon shoveling the snow off the sidewalk or driveway?

7. He shoveled the snow from the front steps to the _____.

8. What did Damon say when he looked back at the sidewalk?

9. What had happened to the sidewalk?

10. If it doesn't stop snowing, will Damon ever get the sidewalk clean?

B. Look at the picture and retell the story.

LISTENING, UNDERSTANDING, REMEMBERING, VERBALIZING!

Instructor's Worksheet

Directions: Before beginning, each student should be given a copy of the picture that corresponds to the instructor's worksheet. The students are to look at the picture as they listen to the story being read aloud. Utilizing both the visual and auditory channels simultaneously will aid the students in remembering the details of the story. The students are to answer the questions or complete the sentences as they are read aloud. Finally, the students should look at the picture and retell the story in their own words.

Story #35:

Wally's big brother usually walks the dog. Wally asked his brother if he could hold the leash today. His brother said he could try but he might be too small. Wally took the leash and said, "Let's go, Spot!" Spot started running so fast that Wally was tossed in the air. However, he held on to the leash. Wally's brother grabbed the leash and said to Wally, "Let's hold the leash together and walk Spot."

A. Will you help explain why Wally needed his brother to help walk the dog?

1. Who usually walks the dog?

2. What did Wally want to do today?

3. Did Wally's brother think he was too big or too small to hold the leash?

4. What is the name of Wally's dog?

5. When Wally took the leash, what did he say to Spot?

6. Did Spot start running slowly or fast?

7. What happened to Wally when Spot started running fast?

8. Did Wally let go of the leash?

9. What did Wally's brother do?

10. Who is going to walk the dog now?

B. Look at the picture and retell the story.

35¢

LISTENING, UNDERSTANDING, REMEMBERING,
VERBALIZING!

Instructor's Worksheet

Directions: Before beginning, each student should be given a copy of the picture that corresponds to the instructor's worksheet. The students are to look at the picture as they listen to the story being read aloud. Utilizing both the visual and auditory channels simultaneously will aid the students in remembering the details of the story. The students are to answer the questions or complete the sentences as they are read aloud. Finally, the students should look at the picture and retell the story in their own words.

Story #36:

John is stopped at a tollbooth. John needs a quarter and a dime. He needs it to pay the money at the tollbooth so that he can drive through and go to work. If he does not put the money in the tollbooth basket, the striped bar will not lift up. He tosses the coins in the basket and the bar lifts to let John's car go through.

A. Will you help explain why John needs to pay money at the tollbooth?

1. John is stopped at a _____.

2. Does he need money or stones to put in the tollbooth basket?

3. What coins does John need to put in the tollbooth basket?

4. John pays the toll when he drives to _____.

5. Where is John supposed to put the coins?

6. What happens after he puts the money in the basket?

7. What do you think will happen if he does not put the money in the basket?

8. Does the toll bar raise up or fall down when the money goes in the basket?

9. Does the bar have stripes or polka dots on it?

10. Will John be able to get through to go to work?

B. Look at the picture and retell the story.

Name: _____

Story #33

Story #34

Story #35

Story #36

Instructor's Worksheet   Remembering Stories 33-36

Directions: At the end of four consecutive stories, there is a review to see if facts in the four stories have been retained. Make sure that all four story lessons have been completed before doing the review lesson. The students should have the student page with the pictures in front of them as the questions are being read aloud. Ask each student to point to the picture being talked about. Students should take turns answering the questions.

Story #33

Story #34

Story #35

Story #36

1. What did Scotty see running out of the hose?

2. The water was making a big _____.

3. What did Scotty pick up before he went over to the hose?

4. What did Scotty make out of the water puddle?

5. Did Damon want to shovel the snow before or after his dad came home from work?

6. Where did he get his shovel?

7. Where did Damon start shoveling the snow?

8. If it keeps snowing so hard, will Damon ever finish cleaning the sidewalk?

9. What did Wally want to do today?

10. When Wally took the leash, what did he say to Spot?

11. What happened to Wally when Spot started running fast?

12. What did Wally and his brother decide to do together?

13. What does John need to put in the tollbooth basket?

14. John pays the toll when he drives to _____.

15. What will happen when he puts the money in the basket?

16. Will John be able to drive through the tollbooth?